&

SELF-CARE FOR
BLACK WOMEN

Marya Patrice Sherron

KI PRODUCTIONS

Where every story matters

Printed in the United States of America
ISBN: 978-1-961605-23-7

First Edition

Written, Designed, & Edited by Marya Patrice Sherron

No portion of this book may be reproduced, stored in a
retrieval system, or transmitted in any form or by any
means, electronic, mechanical, photocopy, recording,
scanning, or others without permission from the author. If
you would like permission to use material from the book,
schedule a reading, recording, or class visit, please contact:
maryapatrice@gmail.com.

This Journal Belongs to:

〰〰〰〰〰〰〰〰〰〰〰〰〰

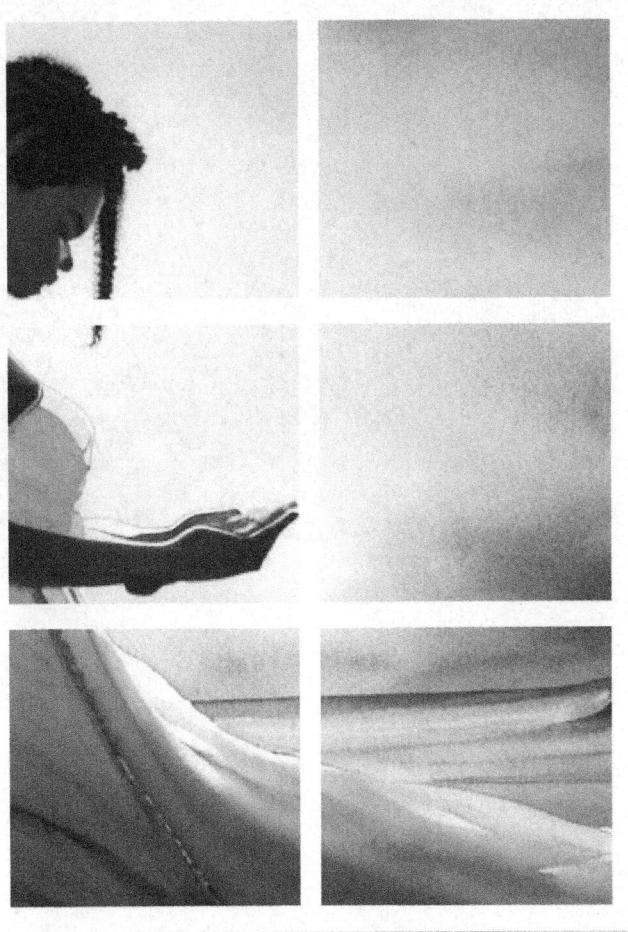

Health

Week 1

Set aside time each day to be with our Lord. It does not matter where— you only need be fully present.

___/___/___
Date

Today's Affirmation

Today's Goals

Sing to the Lord a new song;
sing to the Lord, all the earth.
Sing to the Lord, praise his
name; proclaim his salvation
day after day. Declare his glory
among the nations,
his marvelous deeds
among all peoples.

~ Psalm 96:1-3

_____
_____
_____
_____

Today's Prayer

_____
_____
_____
_____
_____
_____
_____
_____
_____

Self-Care Check

Exercise & Activities

❀ _____

❀ _____

❀ _____

Water Check

How are you?

What is your greatest need right now?

Daily Reflections

_____

_____

_____

_____

_____

_____

_____

_____

_____

_____

_____

_____

_____

Lord, by such things people live; and my spirit finds life in them too.
You restored me to health and let me live.

Isaiah 38:16

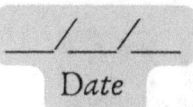
___/___/___
Date

Today's Affirmation

Today's Goals

_____

_____

_____

_____

Today's Prayer

_____

_____

_____

_____

_____

_____

_____

_____

_____

_____

Self-Care Check

Exercise & Activities

❀ _____
❀ _____
❀ _____

Water Check

How are you?

What is your greatest need right now?

Daily Reflections

_____

_____

_____

_____

_____

_____

_____

_____

_____

_____

_____

_____

_____

Nevertheless, I will bring health and healing to it; I will heal my people and will let them enjoy abundant peace and security.

Jeremiah 33:6

___ / ___ / ___
Date

Today's Affirmation

Today's Goals

Sing to the Lord a new song,
for he has done marvelous things;
his right hand and his holy arm
have worked salvation for him.
~ Psalm 98:1

_____
_____
_____
_____

Today's Prayer 🌿

_____
_____
_____
_____
_____
_____
_____
_____
_____
_____
_____

Self-Care Check

Exercise & Activities

✿ _____

✿ _____

✿ _____

Water Check

How are you?

What is your greatest need right now?

Daily Reflections

_____

_____

_____

_____

_____

_____

_____

_____

_____

_____

_____

_____

_____

The eye is the lamp of the body. If your eyes are healthy,
your whole body will be full of light.

Matthew 6:22

__/__/__

Date

Today's Affirmation

Today's Goals

_____
_____
_____
_____

Today's Prayer

_____
_____
_____
_____
_____
_____
_____
_____
_____
_____

Self-Care Check

Exercise & Activities

❀ _____

❀ _____

❀ _____

Water Check

How are you?

What is your greatest need right now?

Daily Reflections

_____
_____
_____
_____
_____
_____
_____
_____
_____
_____
_____
_____
_____
_____

Dear friend, I pray that you may enjoy good health and that all
may go well with you, even as your soul is getting along well.

3 John 1:2

No matter how many times you fall, how many 'nos' or "not good enoughs" you get, never... never give up on that which is pressed upon your heart. Your time will come..

Be there for it.

___/___/___
Date

Today's Affirmation

Today's Goals

And they sang a new song, saying:
"You are worthy to take the scroll
and to open its seals,
because you were slain,
and with your blood you
purchased for God
persons from every tribe and
language and people and nation."
~ Revelation 5:9

_____

_____

_____

_____

Today's Prayer

Self-Care Check

Exercise & Activities

Water Check

How are you?

What is your greatest need right now?

Daily Reflections

_____

_____

_____

_____

_____

_____

_____

_____

_____

_____

_____

_____

_____

_____

Restore to me the joy of your salvation and grant me a willing spirit,
to sustain me.

Psalm 51:12

___/___/___

Date

Today's Affirmation

Today's Goals

_____

_____

_____

_____

Today's Prayer

_____

_____

_____

_____

_____

_____

_____

_____

_____

_____

Self-Care Check

Exercise & Activities

✿ _____

✿ _____

✿ _____

Water Check

How are you?

What is your greatest need right now?

Daily Reflections

_____

_____

_____

_____

_____

_____

_____

_____

_____

_____

_____

_____

_____

_____

Though you have made me see troubles, many and bitter, you will restore my life again; from the depths of the earth you will again bring me up.

Psalm 71:20

__/__/__
Date

Today's Affirmation

Today's Goals

The Lord your God is with you,
the Mighty Warrior who saves.
He will take great delight in you;
in his love he will no longer
rebuke you,
but will rejoice over you with
singing.
~ Zephaniah 3:17

Today's Prayer

Self-Care Check

Exercise & Activities

✿ _____

✿ _____

✿ _____

Water Check

How are you?

What is your greatest need right now?

Daily Reflections

_____
_____
_____
_____
_____
_____
_____
_____
_____
_____
_____
_____
_____

*Seek a verse to reflect on today.*_____

Perhaps this is the
moment for which
you have been
created.

Esther 4:14

Rest

Week

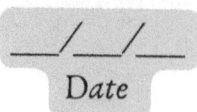
___/___/___
Date

Today's Affirmation

Today's Goals

_____
_____
_____
_____

Today's Prayer

_____
_____
_____
_____
_____
_____
_____
_____
_____
_____

Self-Care Check

Exercise & Activities

🌸 _____

🌸 _____

🌸 _____

Water Check

How are you?

What is your greatest need right now?

Daily Reflections

_____
_____
_____
_____
_____
_____
_____
_____
_____
_____
_____
_____
_____
_____

Whoever dwells in the shelter of the Most High will rest in the shadow of the Almighty.

Psalm 91

__/__/__

Date

Today's Affirmation

Today's Goals

Let the message of Christ dwell among you richly as you teach and admonish one another with all wisdom through psalms, hymns, and songs from the Spirit, singing to God with gratitude in your hearts.

~ Colossians 3:16

_____
_____
_____
_____

Today's Prayer

_____
_____
_____
_____
_____
_____
_____
_____
_____

Self-Care Check

Exercise & Activities

❀ _____

❀ _____

❀ _____

Water Check

How are you?

What is your greatest need right now?

Daily Reflections

_____
_____
_____
_____
_____
_____
_____
_____
_____
_____
_____
_____
_____
_____
_____
_____
_____
_____

Seek a verse to reflect on today.   *Scripture:* _____

___/___/___
Date

Today's Affirmation

Today's Goals

_____

_____

_____

_____

Today's Prayer

_____

_____

_____

_____

_____

_____

_____

_____

_____

Self-Care Check

Exercise & Activities

✿ _____

✿ _____

✿ _____

Water Check

How are you?

What is your greatest need right now?

Daily Reflections

_____

_____

_____

_____

_____

_____

_____

_____

_____

_____

_____

_____

Praise be to the Lord, who has given rest to his people Israel just as he promised. Not one word has failed of all the good promises he gave through his servant Moses.

1 Kings 8:56

___/___/___
Date

Today's Affirmation

Today's Goals

Because your love is better than
life, my lips will glorify you. I will
praise you as long as I live, and in
your name I will lift up my hands.
~Psalm 63:3-4

_____

_____

_____

_____

Today's Prayer

Self-Care Check

Exercise & Activities

🌼 _____

🌼 _____

🌼 _____

Water Check

How are you?

What is your greatest need right now?

Daily Reflections

_____
_____
_____
_____
_____
_____
_____
_____
_____
_____
_____
_____
_____
_____
_____

Seek a verse to reflect on today.   Scripture: _____

___/___/___
Date

Today's Affirmation

Today's Goals

_____
_____
_____
_____

Today's Prayer

_____
_____
_____
_____
_____
_____
_____
_____
_____
_____

Self-Care Check

Exercise & Activities

❀ _____

❀ _____

❀ _____

Water Check

How are you?

What is your greatest need right now?

Daily Reflections

_____

_____

_____

_____

_____

_____

_____

_____

_____

_____

_____

_____

_____

_____

_____

Seek a verse to reflect on today.   *Scripture:* _____

Have I not commanded
you? Be strong and
courageous. Do not be
frightened, and do not be
dismayed, for the LORD
your God is with you
wherever you go.

Joshua 1:9

Write *a daily affirmation.*

Write your own quote or inspiring word or phrase in your wreath.

___/___/___
Date

Today's Affirmation

Today's Goals

_____
_____
_____
_____

Today's Prayer

_____
_____
_____
_____
_____
_____
_____
_____
_____

Self-Care Check

Exercise & Activities

✿ _____

✿ _____

✿ _____

Water Check

How are you?

What is your greatest need right now?

Daily Reflections

_____
_____
_____
_____
_____
_____
_____
_____
_____
_____
_____
_____
_____
_____
_____

Come to me, all you who are weary and burdened, and I will give you
rest.

Matthew 11:28

You're a big deal.

Remember that.

Patience

Week 3

___/___/___
Date

Today's Affirmation

Today's Goals

*I cried out to him with my
mouth; his praise was on
my tongue.*
~ Psalm 66:17

_____
_____
_____
_____

Today's Prayer

Self-Care Check

Exercise & Activities

🌸 _____

🌸 _____

🌸 _____

Water Check

How are you?

What is your greatest need right now?

Daily Reflections

_____
_____
_____
_____
_____
_____
_____
_____
_____
_____
_____
_____
_____

We do not want you to become lazy, but to imitate those who through faith and patience inherit what has been promised.

Hebrews 6:12

___/___/___
Date

Today's Affirmation

Today's Goals

_____

_____

_____

_____

Today's Prayer

_____

_____

_____

_____

_____

_____

_____

_____

_____

_____

Self-Care Check

Exercise & Activities

✿ _____

✿ _____

✿ _____

Water Check

How are you?

What is your greatest need right now?

Daily Reflections

_____

_____

_____

_____

_____

_____

_____

_____

_____

_____

_____

_____

_____

_____

Seek a verse to reflect on today.   *Scripture:* _____

___/___/___
Date

Today's Affirmation

Today's Goals

*You are my hiding place; you
will protect me from trouble
and surround me with
songs of deliverance.*
~ Psalm 32:7

Today's Prayer

Self-Care Check

Exercise & Activities

❀ _____

❀ _____

❀ _____

Water Check

How are you?

What is your greatest need right now?

Daily Reflections

---

*Therefore, as God's chosen people, holy and dearly loved, clothe yourselves with
compassion, kindness, humility, gentleness and patience.*

Colossians 3:12

___/___/___

Date

Today's Affirmation

Today's Goals

_____
_____
_____
_____

Today's Prayer

_____
_____
_____
_____
_____
_____
_____
_____
_____
_____

Self-Care Check

Exercise & Activities

- ✿ _____
- ✿ _____
- ✿ _____

Water Check

How are you?

What is your greatest need right now?

Daily Reflections

_____

_____

_____

_____

_____

_____

_____

_____

_____

_____

_____

_____

_____

The end of a matter is better than its beginning, and patience is better than pride.

Ecclesiastes 7:8

_____/_____/_____

Date

Today's Affirmation

Today's Goals

Then Moses and the Israelites sang this song to the Lord:
"I will sing to the Lord,
  for he is highly exalted.
Both horse and driver
  he has hurled into the sea.
"The Lord is my strength and my defense;
  he has become my salvation.
He is my God, and I will praise him,
  my father's God, and I will exalt him.
The Lord is a warrior;
  the Lord is his name."

~ Exodus 15:1-3

Today's Prayer

Self-Care Check

Exercise & Activities

Water Check

How are you?

What is your greatest need right now?

Daily Reflections

_____
_____
_____
_____
_____
_____
_____
_____
_____
_____
_____
_____
_____
_____
_____

Seek a verse to reflect on today.   Scripture: _____

___/___/___

Date

Today's Affirmation

Today's Goals

_____
_____
_____
_____

Today's Prayer

_____
_____
_____
_____
_____
_____
_____
_____
_____

Self-Care Check

Exercise & Activities

❀ _____

❀ _____

❀ _____

Water Check

How are you?

What is your greatest need right now?

Daily Reflections

_____

_____

_____

_____

_____

_____

_____

_____

_____

_____

_____

_____

_____

You know the message God sent to the people of Israel, announcing the good
news of peace through Jesus Christ, who is Lord of all.

Acts 10:36

_____/_____/_____

Date

Today's Affirmation

Today's Goals

*About midnight Paul and Silas
were praying and singing hymns to
God, and the other prisoners were
listening to them.*

~ Acts 16:25

_____
_____
_____
_____

Today's Prayer

Self-Care Check

Exercise & Activities

❀ _____

❀ _____

❀ _____

Water Check

How are you?

What is your greatest need right now?

Daily Reflections

_____

_____

_____

_____

_____

_____

_____

_____

_____

_____

_____

_____

_____

_____

_____

_____

*And the peace of God, which transcends all understanding, will guard your
hearts and your minds in Christ Jesus.*

Philippians 4:7

May the God of hope fill you with all joy and
peace as you trust in Him, so that you may
overflow with hope by the power of the
Holy Spirit.

Romans 15:13

Joy

Week 4

___/___/___

Date

Today's Affirmation

Today's Goals

_____
_____
_____
_____

Today's Prayer

_____
_____
_____
_____
_____
_____
_____
_____
_____

Self-Care Check

Exercise & Activities

❁ _____

❁ _____

❁ _____

Water Check

How are you?

What is your greatest need right now?

Daily Reflections

_____

_____

_____

_____

_____

_____

_____

_____

_____

_____

_____

_____

_____

_____

A person finds joy in giving an apt reply— and how good is a timely word.
Proverbs 15:23

___/___/___
Date

Today's Affirmation

Today's Goals

I will sing a new song to you,
my God; On the ten-stringed
lyre I will make music to you,
~ Psalm 144:9

Today's Prayer

Self-Care Check

Exercise & Activities

❀ _____

❀ _____

❀ _____

Water Check

How are you?

What is your greatest need right now?

Daily Reflections

_____

_____

_____

_____

_____

_____

_____

_____

_____

_____

_____

_____

_____

_____

*Perfume and incense bring joy to the heart, and the pleasantness of a
friend springs from their heartfelt advice.*

Proverbs 27:9

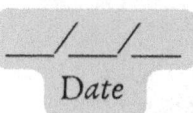
___/___/___
Date

Today's Affirmation

Today's Goals

_____

_____

_____

_____

Today's Prayer

Self-Care Check

Exercise & Activities

❀ _____

❀ _____

❀ _____

Water Check

How are you?

What is your greatest need right now?

Daily Reflections

_____

_____

_____

_____

_____

_____

_____

_____

_____

_____

_____

_____

_____

_____

_____

_____

_____

Seek a verse to reflect on today.   *Scripture:* _____

___/___/___
Date

Today's Affirmation

Today's Goals

...speaking to one another with psalms, hymns, and songs from the Spirit. Sing and make music from your heart to the Lord,

~ Ephesians 5:19

_____
_____
_____
_____

Today's Prayer

_____
_____
_____
_____
_____
_____
_____
_____
_____

Self-Care Check

Exercise & Activities

❀ _____

❀ _____

❀ _____

Water Check

How are you?

What is your greatest need right now?

Daily Reflections

_____

_____

_____

_____

_____

_____

_____

_____

_____

_____

_____

_____

_____

_____

_____

_____

*May the God of hope fill you with all joy and peace as you trust in him, so that
you may overflow with hope by the power of the Holy Spirit.*

Romans 15:13

___/___/___

Date

Today's Affirmation

Today's Goals

_____

_____

_____

_____

Today's Prayer

_____

_____

_____

_____

_____

_____

_____

_____

_____

Self-Care Check

Exercise & Activities

❀ _____

❀ _____

❀ _____

Water Check

How are you?

What is your greatest need right now?

Daily Reflections

Yet I will rejoice in the Lord, I will be joyful in God my Savior.
Habakkuk 3:18

___/___/___

Date

Today's Affirmation

Today's Goals

He *put a new song in my mouth,*
a hymn of praise to our God.
Many will see and fear the Lord
and put their trust in him.
~ Psalm 40:1

Today's Prayer

Self-Care Check

Exercise & Activities

❀ _____

❀ _____

❀ _____

Water Check

How are you?

What is your greatest need right now?

Daily Reflections

_____

_____

_____

_____

_____

_____

_____

_____

_____

_____

_____

_____

_____

But the angel said to them, "Do not be afraid. I bring you good news that will cause great joy for all the people."

Luke 2:10

_____/_____/_____
Date

Today's Affirmation

Today's Goals

_____
_____
_____
_____

Today's Prayer

Self-Care Check

Exercise & Activities

Water Check

How are you?

What is your greatest need right now?

Daily Reflections

_____

_____

_____

_____

_____

_____

_____

_____

_____

_____

_____

_____

_____

_____

_____

You have loved righteousness and hated wickedness; therefore God, your God,
has set you above your companions by anointing you with the oil of joy.

Hebrews 1:9

Love

Week

___/___/___
Date

Today's Affirmation

Today's Goals

Sing to the Lord a new song,
his praise from the ends
of the earth,
you who go down to the sea,
and all that is in it,
you islands, and all who
live in them.
~ Isaiah 42:10

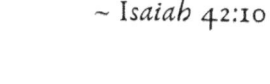

_____
_____
_____
_____

Today's Prayer

_____
_____
_____
_____
_____
_____
_____
_____
_____

Self-Care Check

Exercise & Activities

🌸 _____

🌸 _____

🌸 _____

Water Check

How are you?

What is your greatest need right now?

Daily Reflections

_____
_____
_____
_____
_____
_____
_____
_____
_____
_____
_____
_____
_____
_____
_____
_____

Seek a verse to reflect on today.   *Scripture:* _____

___/___/___
Date

Today's Affirmation

Today's Goals

Today's Prayer

Self-Care Check

Exercise & Activities

🌸 _____

🌸 _____

🌸 _____

Water Check

How are you?

What is your greatest need right now?

Daily Reflections

_____

_____

_____

_____

_____

_____

_____

_____

_____

_____

_____

_____

_____

_____

love _____.

___/___/___
Date

Today's Affirmation

Today's Goals

Because I rescued the poor who cried for help, and the fatherless who had none to assist them. The one who was dying blessed me; I made the widow's heart sing.
~ Job 29:12-13

_____
_____
_____
_____

Today's Prayer

_____
_____
_____
_____
_____
_____
_____
_____
_____
_____

Self-Care Check

Exercise & Activities

✿ _____

✿ _____

✿ _____

Water Check

How are you?

What is your greatest need right now?

Daily Reflections

_____
_____
_____
_____
_____
_____
_____
_____
_____
_____
_____
_____
_____
_____
_____

Seek a verse to reflect on today.   *Scripture:* _____

___/___/___
Date

Today's Affirmation

Today's Goals

Today's Prayer

Self-Care Check

Exercise & Activities

❀ _____

❀ _____

❀ _____

Water Check

How are you?

What is your greatest need right now?

Daily Reflections

_____
_____
_____
_____
_____
_____
_____
_____
_____
_____
_____
_____
_____

The Ephraimites will become like warriors, and their hearts will be glad as with wine. Their children will see it and be joyful; their hearts will rejoice in the Lord.
Zechariah 10:7

____/____/____
Date

Today's Affirmation

Today's Goals

He says, "I will declare
your name to my
brothers and sisters; in
the assembly I will sing
your praises."
~ Hebrews 2:12

_____
_____
_____
_____

Today's Prayer 🌿

_____
_____
_____
_____
_____
_____
_____
_____
_____

Self-Care Check

Exercise & Activities

❀ _____

❀ _____

❀ _____

Water Check

How are you?

What is your greatest need right now?

Daily Reflections

Go, eat your food with gladness, and drink your wine with a joyful heart, for God has already approved what you do.

Ecclesiastes 9:7

_____/_____/_____

Date

Today's Affirmation

Today's Goals

Today's Prayer 🌿

Self-Care Check

Exercise & Activities

❀ _____

❀ _____

❀ _____

Water Check

How are you?

What is your greatest need right now?

Daily Reflections

_____

_____

_____

_____

_____

_____

_____

_____

_____

_____

_____

_____

*I have told you this so that my joy may be in you and that your
joy may be complete.*

John 15:11

I declare
that my heart
be filled
with thanksgiving
and praise for all
His goodness
in my life.

_____/_____/_____
Date

Today's Affirmation

Today's Goals

My lips will shout for joy
when I sing praise to you
— I whom you have
delivered.
~ Psalm 71:23

_____

_____

_____

_____

Today's Prayer

_____

_____

_____

_____

_____

_____

_____

_____

_____

Self-Care Check

Exercise & Activities

❀ _____
❀ _____
❀ _____

Water Check

How are you?

What is your greatest need right now?

Daily Reflections

_____

_____

_____

_____

_____

_____

_____

_____

_____

_____

_____

_____

_____

Instead, speaking the truth in love, we will grow to become in every respect the mature body of him who is the head, that is, Christ.

Ephesians 4:15

Compassion

Week 6

___/___/___
Date

Today's Affirmation

Today's Goals

_____

_____

_____

_____

Today's Prayer

_____

_____

_____

_____

_____

_____

_____

_____

_____

_____

Self-Care Check

Exercise & Activities

❀ _____

❀ _____

❀ _____

Water Check

How are you?

What is your greatest need right now?

Daily Reflections

Very truly I tell you, you will weep and mourn while the world rejoices. You will grieve, but your grief will turn to joy.

John 16:20

___/___/___
Date

Today's Affirmation

Today's Goals

I will sing of your love
and justice; to you,
LORD, I will sing praise.
~ Psalm 101:1

_____
_____
_____
_____

Today's Prayer

_____
_____
_____
_____
_____
_____
_____
_____
_____
_____

Self-Care Check

Exercise & Activities

❀ _____

❀ _____

❀ _____

Water Check

How are you?

What is your greatest need right now?

Daily Reflections

_____

_____

_____

_____

_____

_____

_____

_____

_____

_____

_____

_____

_____

_____

_____

_____

But God demonstrates his own love for us in this: While we were still sinners,
Christ died for us.

Romans 5:8

___/___/___
Date

Today's Affirmation

Today's Goals

Today's Prayer

_____
_____
_____
_____
_____
_____
_____
_____
_____
_____

Self-Care Check

Exercise & Activities

✿ _____

✿ _____

✿ _____

Water Check

How are you?

What is your greatest need right now?

Daily Reflections

_____

_____

_____

_____

_____

_____

_____

_____

_____

_____

_____

_____

_____

_____

_____

Love must be sincere. Hate what is evil; cling to what is good.
Be devoted to one another in love. Honor one another above yourselves.

Romans 12:10

_____ / _____ / _____
Date

Today's Affirmation

Today's Goals

Praise the LORD. Praise God in his
sanctuary; praise him in his mighty heavens.
Praise him for his acts of power; praise him
for his surpassing greatness.
Praise him with the sounding of the trumpet,
praise him with the harp and lyre,
praise him with timbrel and dancing, praise
him with the strings and pipe,
praise him with the clash of cymbals, praise
him with resounding cymbals.
~ Psalm 150:1-5

Today's Prayer

Self-Care Check

Exercise & Activities

✿ _____

✿ _____

✿ _____

Water Check

How are you?

What is your greatest need right now?

Daily Reflections

_____

_____

_____

_____

_____

_____

_____

_____

_____

_____

_____

_____

_____

Flee the evil desires of youth and pursue righteousness, faith, love and peace, along with those who call on the Lord out of a pure heart.

2 Timothy 2:22

___/___/___
Date

Today's Affirmation

Today's Goals

I will be glad and rejoice in you; I will sing the praises of your name, O Most High.

~ Psalm 9:2

Today's Prayer 🌿

Self-Care Check

Exercise & Activities

- ✿ _____
- ✿ _____
- ✿ _____

Water Check

How are you?

What is your greatest need right now?

Daily Reflections

Be completely humble and gentle; be patient, bearing with one another in love.

Ephesians 4:2

Today's Affirmation

Today's Goals

Sing to the LORD a new song, for he has done
marvelous things; his right hand and his holy
arm have worked salvation for him.
The LORD has made his salvation known
and revealed his righteousness to the nations.
He has remembered his love and his
faithfulness to Israel; all the ends of the earth
have seen the salvation of our God.
Shout for joy to the LORD, all the earth,
burst into jubilant song with music;
make music to the LORD with the harp, with
the harp and the sound of singing,
with trumpets and the blast of the ram's horn
— shout for joy before the LORD, the King.
Let the sea resound, and everything in it, the
world, and all who live in it.

~ Psalm 98:1-7

_____

_____

_____

_____

Today's Prayer

_____

_____

_____

_____

_____

_____

_____

_____

_____

_____

Self-Care Check

Exercise & Activities

❀ _____
❀ _____
❀ _____

Water Check

How are you?

What is your greatest need right now?

Daily Reflections

_____

_____

_____

_____

_____

_____

_____

_____

_____

_____

_____

_____

_____

_____

*From him the whole body, joined and held together by every supporting
ligament, grows and builds itself up in love, as each part does its work.*

Ephesians 4:16

To laugh
at yourself
is to love
yourself

Use the following page to
write a love letter to
yourself. Take time to
acknowledge all you have
overcome, your gifts, your
kindness toward others, and
what makes you special.

Women of the Bible to Read About For Encouragement

The Bleeding Woman - Matt 9; Mark 5

Queen Esther - Esther

Gomer - Hosea 1-3

The Woman at the Well - John 4

Tabitha - Acts 9

Naomi & Ruth - Ruth

Tamar - Genesis 38

Rahab - Joshua 2-3; Hebrews 11; James 2

Hannah - 1 Samuel 1 & 2

Deborah - Judges 4,5; Hebrews 11

I sought the LORD, *and* He answered me and delivered me from all my fears. Those who look to Him are radiant, and their faces shall never be ashamed. Oh, taste and see that the LORD *is good!* Blessed is the man who takes refuge in Him!

Psalm 34:4-5,8

Made in United States
Orlando, FL
25 November 2024

54488546R00104